D1164554

THERE IS NO RIGHT WAY TO MEDITATE
AND OTHER LESSONS

yumi Sakugawa

Adams Media
New York London Toronto Sydney New Delhi

Adams Media
An Imprint of Simon & Schuster, Inc.
57 Littlefield Street
Avon, Massachusetts 02322

For information about special discounts for bulk purchases, please contact Simon & Schuster Special Sales at 1-866-506-1949 or business@simonand-schuster.com.

The Simon & Schuster Speakers Bureau can bring authors to your live event. For more information or to book an event contact the Simon & Schuster Speakers Bureau at 1-866-248-3049 or visit our website at www.simonspeakers.com.

Cover and interior illustrations by Yumi Sakugawa

Manufactured in the United States of America

10 9 8 7 6 5 4 3 2

Library of Congress Cataloging-in-Publication Data has been applied for.

ISBN 978-1-4405-9252-2
ISBN 978-1-4405-9253-9 (ebook)

WHEN I WAS 23 YEARS OLD AND DEPRESSED OUT OF MY
MIND, I HAD THE LIFE-CHANGING EPHIPHANY
THAT I AM NOT MY THOUGHTS - BUT RATHER,
THE SPACE IN BETWEEN MY THOUGHTS.

WHAT A PROFOUND RELIEF IT WAS TO DISCOVER FOR THE
FIRST TIME EVER IN MY LIFE THAT ALL
MY ANXIOUS, NEUROTIC, SELF-
LOATHING THOUGHTS ABOUT
MYSELF COULD SIMPLY DRIFT PAST ME,
FORMLESS AND INCONSEQUENTIAL AS CLOUDS MOVING
ACROSS THE SKY.

MAKING COMICS ABOUT MEDITATION AND MINDFULNESS
IS MY OWN WAY OF ANCHORING MYSELF DEEPER INTO
MY PRACTICE, TO VISUALLY ARTICULATE FOR MYSELF
AND FOR OTHERS WHAT IT MEANS TO EMBODY THE
EMPTINESS AND INNER SILENCE THAT CREATE
OPENINGS FOR YOUR TRUE ESSENCE TO SHINE
THROUGH.

I HOPE THAT IN READING THIS BOOK YOU, TOO,
WILL ALSO BE REMINDED OF YOUR OWN INNER
LIGHT, YOUR OWN INFINITE TRUE SELF.

YUMI SAKUGAWA 2015

THIS IS YOUR MIND

THIS IS YOUR MIND ON MEDITATION.
ANY QUESTIONS

10 WAYS TO GET RID OF YOUR BAD MOOD

① HAVE YOUR DOPPELGÄNGER EXTRACT YOUR BAD MOOD FROM YOUR CHEST SO HE/SHE CAN MAKE FUN SCULPTURES WITH IT

ta·dah

② PAINT OUT YOUR BAD MOOD. WHEN YOU'RE FINISHED WITH YOUR PAINTING, SET IT ON FIRE

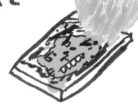

③ EXPLAIN THE REASONS FOR YOUR BAD MOOD OVER A CUP OF TEA — WITH YOUR TWO-HEADED NEIGHBORS

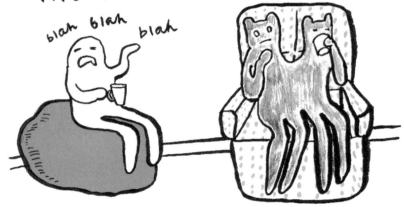

⑤ TURN YOUR BODY INSIDE-OUT SO YOUR BAD MOOD FALLS OUT ONTO THE GROUND

BREATHE OUT YOUR
BAD MOOD

AND WATCH IT
DISAPPEAR
INTO THE SKY

⑧ BEAT YOUR BAD MOOD
IN A STARING CONTEST
SO IT SLINKS AWAY
IN DEFEAT

⑨ FREAK OUT YOUR BAD MOOD BY ACTING ALL SUPER-FAKE AND CHUMMY WITH IT

COME ON, LET'S GO WATCH A MOVIE

UH... IT'S OK.

⑩ (*your amazing idea here* ) **PLEASE SHARE**

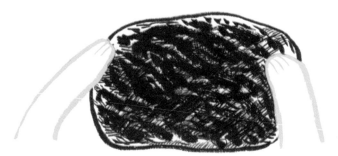

BUT SOMETIMES, IF YOU TAKE THE TIME TO FEEL THE TEXTURE AND RIDGES OF YOUR ANXIETY......

IT FEELS JUST A LITTLE LESS HEAVY THAN IT WAS BEFORE.

a simple illustrated guided meditation

① SIT IN A COMFORTABLE POSITION.

② FEEL THE WEIGHT OF THE AIR AROUND YOU.

③ FEEL THE SURFACE OF YOUR OWN SKIN.

④ NOW IMAGINE THAT A MAGICAL ERASER IS ERASING THE OUTLINE OF YOUR BEING...

⑤ UNTIL THERE IS NO BOUNDARY BETWEEN YOU AND THE REST OF THE UNIVERSE. OM.

THE END

HOW TO AVOID THE NEGATIVE ENERGY OF OTHER PEOPLE

① ALWAYS HAVE AN IMAGINARY BODYGUARD BY YOUR SIDE TO FIGHT OFF NEGATIVE ENERGY WAVES OF NEGATIVE PEOPLE.

② EVERY JERK MONSTER HAS A SAD HUMAN BEING INSIDE. REMEMBER THIS.

THE NEXT TIME A JERK MONSTER BUGS YOU, CONSCIOUSLY SEND COMPASSIONATE ENERGY TO THE SAD HUMAN BEING TRAPPED INSIDE.

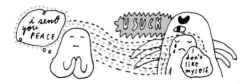

③ WEAR AN EAR PIECE THAT TRANSLATES
THE JERK MONSTER'S WORDS INTO ITS
OPPOSITE MEANING.

④ A NEGATIVE NANCY JUST HAS TO
DUMP HER ENERGY ONTO JUST ANYBODY.
DON'T TAKE IT PERSONALLY, IT HAS
NOTHING TO DO WITH YOU.

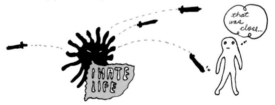

⑤ WEAR A MAGICAL MIRROR SUIT SO THE
NEGATIVE PERSON'S TOXIC ENERGY
SIMPLY BOUNCES BACK TO THE
PERSON AND DOESN'T AFFECT YOU
AT ALL.

SEVEN SIMPLE WAYS TO PRACTICE PEACE

GIVE SOMEONE A PAPER CRANE

LIGHT A CANDLE FOR THE COUNTLESS WOMEN, MEN, AND CHILDREN WHO HAVE GIVEN THEIR LIVES FOR PEACE

READ A NEW
BOOK ABOUT PEACE — WHETHER
IT IS AN AUTOBIOGRAPHY OR ABOUT
YOUR FAVORITE SPIRITUAL AUTHOR

IMAGINE
WHAT A PEACEFUL
WORLD LOOKS
LIKE — NO MATTER
HOW FAR-FETCHED
IT MAY SEEM

SEND A CARD TO A LOVED ONE WHO IS STRESSED OR OVERWHELMED

DONATE TIME/ MONEY TO A CAUSE THAT IS DOING GOOD IN THIS WORLD

SPEND AT LEAST
TEN MINUTES
EVERY DAY
SHOWERING
YOURSELF
WITH SELF-LOVE

(because all
peace starts
with you)

BREATHE IN

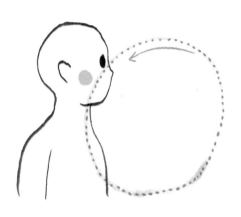

BREATHE OUT

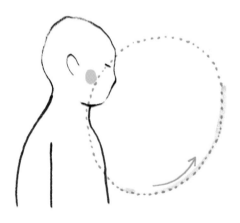

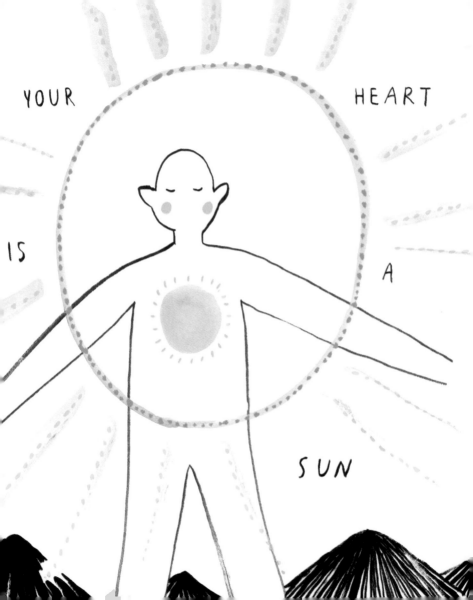

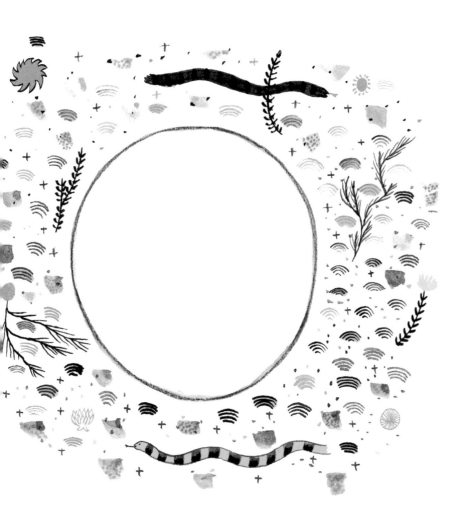

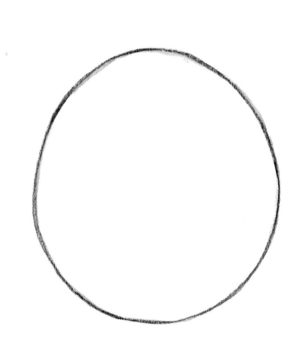

WHY MEDITATION IS GOOD FOR YOU

① YOU FEEL WAY MORE CHILLED OUT... (AND HAPPIER, TOO)

② YOU DON'T FREAK OUT AS MUCH TO LIFE'S INCONVENIENCES AND DETOURS

YOU'RE GOING TO BE LATE? IT'S COOL.

OM

③ CREATIVITY AND NEW IDEAS FLOW INTO YOUR BRAIN WITH GREATER EASE

(MEDITATION IS MAJOR ++++ FOR CREATIVE PEOPLE)

④ LIFE FEELS MORE LIKE RIDING OUT A CURRENT THAN FIGHTING AN UPHILL BATTLE

⑤ AN OVERALL GREATER SENSE OF INNER PEACE AND WHOLENESS

DON'T DWELL ON THE FUTURE

THE FUTURE

THE NEXT TIME YOU ARE FEELING UNHAPPY OR UNCERTAIN, DON'T LOOK HERE, OR HERE

THE PAST

BUT HERE (INSIDE UR ♥) RIGHT HERE AND RIGHT NOW

HOW TO BE A SILENT WITNESS TO YOUR THOUGHTS

an illustrated guide

STEP 1: BE AWARE OF THE FACT THAT YOU ARE THINKING THOUGHTS

i am thinking thoughts

I AM THINKING THAT *i am thinking thoughts*

STEP 2: **NOW DETACH FROM YOURSELF** LIKE YOU ARE HAVING AN OUT-OF-THE-BODY EXPERIENCE

thoughts

YOU ARE NOW BEING THE SILENT WITNESS TO YOUR THOUGHTS

STEP 3: ONCE YOU HAVE DETACHED FROM YOURSELF, OBSERVE YOUR OWN THOUGHTS AS THOUGH YOU ARE A SCIENTIST OBSERVING A LAB SPECIMEN

thoughts

YOU MAY FIND THAT A LOT OF YOUR THOUGHTS ARE QUITE UNPRODUCTIVE AND ACTUALLY HINDER YOUR HAPPINESS

my thoughts — grudges — PARANOIA — I'M FAT — my gift sucks — blah blah blah

STEP 4: TAKE OUT YOUR NEGATIVE THOUGHT PATTERNS AND REPLACE WITH THOUGHTS THAT MAKE YOU HAPPY

my thoughts — I AM THANKFUL AND HAPPY TO BE ALIVE

WE ARE ALL
ONE CRAZY
CONNECTED
WEB

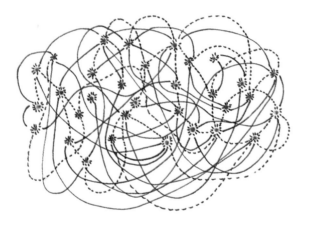

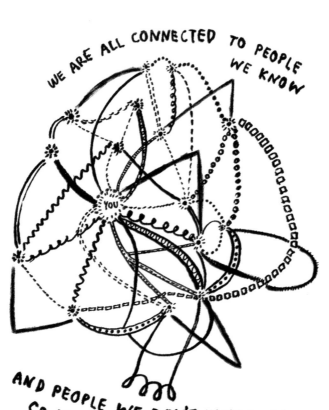

WE ARE ALL CONNECTED TO PEOPLE WE KNOW

YOU

AND PEOPLE WE DON'T KNOW IN SO MANY UNCANNY WAYS BECAUSE NO ONE IS TRULY ALONE

AND YOU AFFECT
THE ENTIRE WEB—
ITS SHAPE, ITS STRUCTURE,
ITS ENERGY

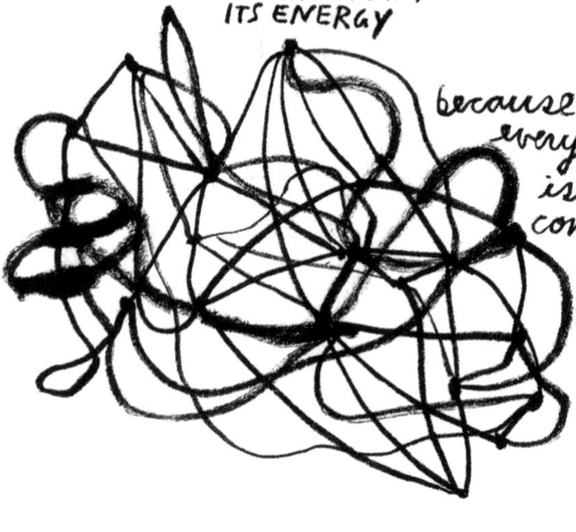

because
everything
is
connected
to
everything

THE END

HOW TO JUST BE

STEP ONE:
FEEL YOURSELF
BREATHING

STEP TWO:
FEEL THE LIGHT
PRESSURE OF
YOUR HEART
BEATING AGAINST
YOUR RIBCAGE

STEP THREE:
FEEL THE EMPTY
SPACE BEHIND
YOUR EYEBALLS

STEP FOUR:
FEEL YOU AS
JUST YOU
BEING YOU
AND BE OKAY
WITH IT

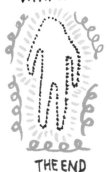

THE END

SKY MEDITATION

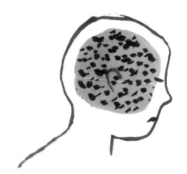

YOU ARE NOT

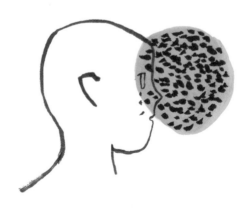

YOUR THOUGHTS

THEY ARE CLOUDS

PASSING BY

AND YOU ARE

THE SKY

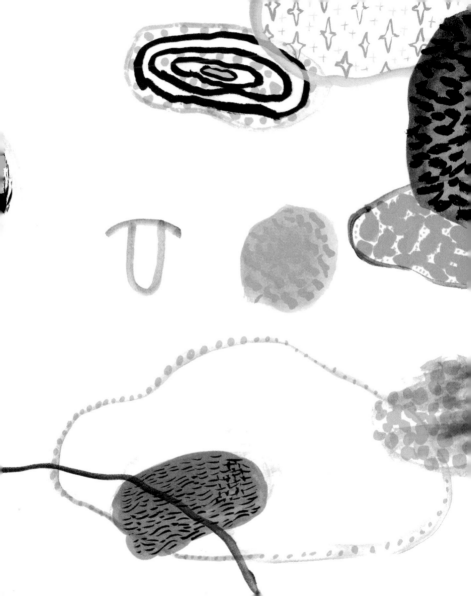

HOW TO MAKE YOUR INTENTIONS COME TRUE

an illustrated guide

STEP 1

THINK OF AN INTENTION YOU WANT TO MANIFEST.

FALL IN LOVE

WRITE A BOOK

RUN A MARATHON

my intention is to...

STEP 2

NOW REALLY VISUALIZE YOURSELF MANIFESTING THAT INTENTION, FROM START TO FINISH, AND THE EMOTIONS THAT ACCOMPANY EACH STEP (ESPECIALLY THE END!).

STEP 3
NOW TAKE THOSE INTENTIONS LIKE SEEDS AND PLANT THEM IN YOUR INNER GARDEN.

PLANT THEM LIKE YOU MEAN IT.

STEP 4

TRUST AND LET GO.
LET THE UNIVERSE
DO THE REST.
AND JUST LIVE
YOUR LIFE AS IS.

WHEN IT IS TIME,
ENJOY THE FRUITS
OF YOUR LIFE'S
HARVEST.

STILL POND MEDITATION

DESIRE

WITHOUT

MINDFULNESS

DESIRE

WITH

MINDFULNESS

RIGHT

NEED

TO

BE

DOES DEATH HAVE ANY ADVICE TODAY?

HOW TO
LISTEN TO
THE SPACES
BETWEEN
YOUR
THOUGHTS

STEP ONE:

i'm so busy these days i don't have the time

LISTEN TO YOUR THOUGHTS

STEP TWO:

i'm hungry right now

I'M HUNGRY RIGHT NOW. I REALLY WANT SOME FISH TACOS BUT THERE'S

IMAGINE YOUR THOUGHTS BEING TRANSCRIBED ON A GIANT SCREEN AS YOU ARE THINKING THEM

STEP THREE:

NOTICE THE SPACES BETWEEN YOUR THOUGHTS

NOTHING IN THE FRIDGE. I THINK I NEED TO GET A HAIRCUT SOON. TODAY IS

THE SPACES ARE BRIEF POCKETS OF SILENCE THAT EXIST IN BETWEEN YOUR NEVER-ENDING STREAM OF THOUGHTS

these silent spaces are sacred.

HAVING MORE SPACE IN YOUR THOUGHTS MEANS

YOU HAVE MORE ROOM FOR YOUR TRUE ESSENCE TO SHINE THROUGH

SO START LISTENING TO THE SILENT SPACES IN YOUR THOUGHTS AND ENJOY THE WELLS OF PEACE THAT EXIST WITHIN THEM.

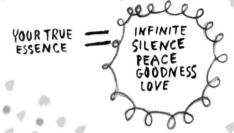

YOUR TRUE
ESSENCE

INFINITE
SILENCE
PEACE
GOODNESS
LOVE

HOW TO REDUCE YOUR PAIN-BODY

(AN ILLUSTRATED GUIDE)

ACCORDING TO SPIRITUAL AUTHOR ECKHART TOLLE, YOUR "PAIN-BODY" IS A PARASITIC ENERGY ENTITY THAT FEEDS ON YOUR NEGATIVITY

IT LIES
DORMANT
INSIDE OF
YOU....

U LOOK
STUPID,
STUPID

UNTIL
SOMETHING
TRIGGERS IT
INTO AN ACTIVE
STATE...

WHICH GIVES IT THE POWER TO TAKE OVER YOUR RATIONALE

AND START FEEDING ON YOUR MISERY

UNTIL IT IS FULLY SATIATED
IT BASICALLY TAKES OVER
YOUR BRAIN, WANTING TO
INFLICT PAIN AND/OR
RECEIVE MORE PAIN
(BASICALLY THE SAME THING)

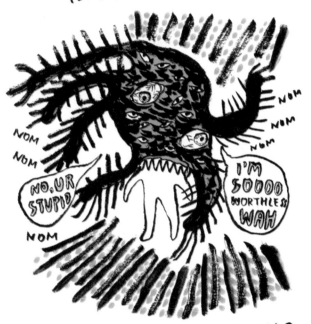

ONCE YOUR PAIN-BODY HAS
ITS FILL, IT GOES BACK TO
ITS DORMANT STATE, WAITING
FOR ITS NEXT OPPORTUNITY...

FORTUNATELY, THERE ARE PROVEN METHODS TO REDUCE YOUR PAIN-BODY

STEP ONE: BE AWARE OF THE FACT THAT YOU HAVE A PAIN-BODY. EVERYONE HAS ONE. PAIN-BODIES HATE SELF-AWARENESS.

STEP TWO: BE FULLY PRESENT WHEN YOUR PAIN-BODY STARTS ACTING UP. KNOW THAT YOU ARE SEPARATE FROM YOUR NEGATIVE SELF-TALK.

PAIIIIN

OH, HELLO AGAIN. YAWN.

(TIP: INTERVIEW YOUR PAIN-BODY WITH VERY BLASÉ QUESTIONS)

SO... WHAT'S GOING ON?

UH.... PAIN?

STEP THREE:
NEVER FIGHT YOUR
PAIN-BODY. JUST
BE A SILENT WITNESS
TO IT AND LET IT
DISAPPEAR ON ITS
OWN...

THERE IS NO RIGHT WAY TO MEDITATE

CONTRARY TO WHAT YOU MAY HAVE HEARD....

THERE ISN'T JUST ONE PERFECT, CORRECT, PURE WAY TO MEDITATE.

MANY PEOPLE LIKE TO SIT IN A COMFORTABLE POSITION WITH THEIR EYES CLOSED

YOU CAN MEDITATE...

IN A CHAIR

ON THE FLOOR

OUTDOORS

IN A BIG GROUP

WITH MUSIC

OTHER PEOPLE LIKE TO MEDITATE

WHILE WALKING

WITH WIDE-OPEN EYES

do what you are most comfortable with

YOU CAN ALSO DECIDE
WHAT YOU WANT TO
FOCUS ON WHEN YOU
ARE MEDITATING...

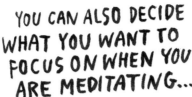

YOUR
FAVORITE
COLOR

I AM LOVE
mantras

AN
IMAGE
THAT
BRINGS
PEACE

YOUR
BREATHING

YOUR
DEITY/
DEITIES

INFINITY

INNER
SILENCE

LOVE

PEACE
for all

THE
SOUND OF
THE OCEAN

YOUR CHAKRAS

A FACE
OF A
LOVED
ONE

SO THE BOTTOM LINE IS THIS:

MEDITATE EVERY DAY – EVEN IF IT MEANS YOU ARE PAYING EXTRA ATTENTION TO THE COLOR OF THE LEAVES FOR 30 SECONDS WHILE WALKING FROM THE POST OFFICE TO YOUR CAR

OR YOU FOCUS ON YOUR BREATHING FOR ONE MINUTE WHILE WAITING FOR YOUR APPOINTMENT AT THE DOCTOR'S OFFICE

SO NO MATTER HOW
BUSY YOU ARE...

SQUEEZE A LITTLE
MEDITATION INTO
YOUR EVERYDAY
SCHEDULE

AND EVERY DAY, YOUR
CAPACITY FOR PEACE,
JOY, AND COMPASSION
GROWS BY JUST A
LITTLE BIT

the end

THE

ROCK

IN

YOUR

HEART

TURN THE ROCK IN
YOUR HEART

INTO A WEB OF FIRE

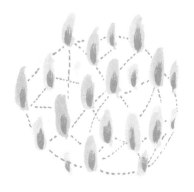

TO
LEAD

YOUR
SELF

OUT
OF

THE

DARKNESS

TURN THE
ROCK IN
YOUR HEART

INTO A RIVER

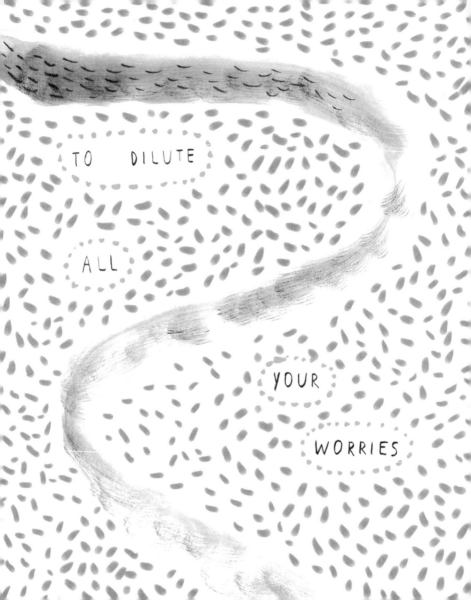

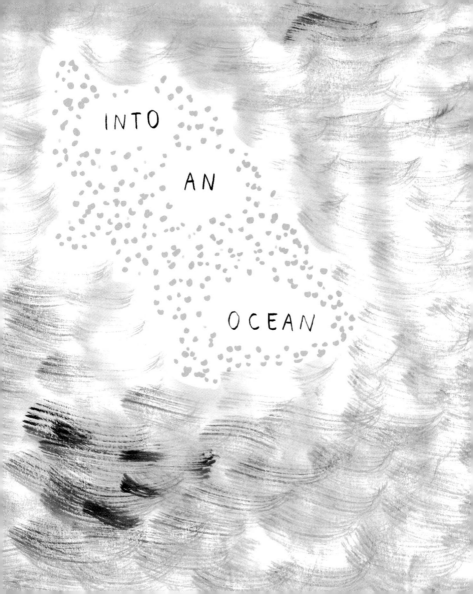

TURN THE
ROCK IN YOUR
HEART

INTO A CRYSTAL

THAT REFLECTS

LIGHT

REMIND THE ROCK IN YOUR HEART

THAT IT IS NOT A ROCK

BUT
A
SEED
IN
DISGUISE

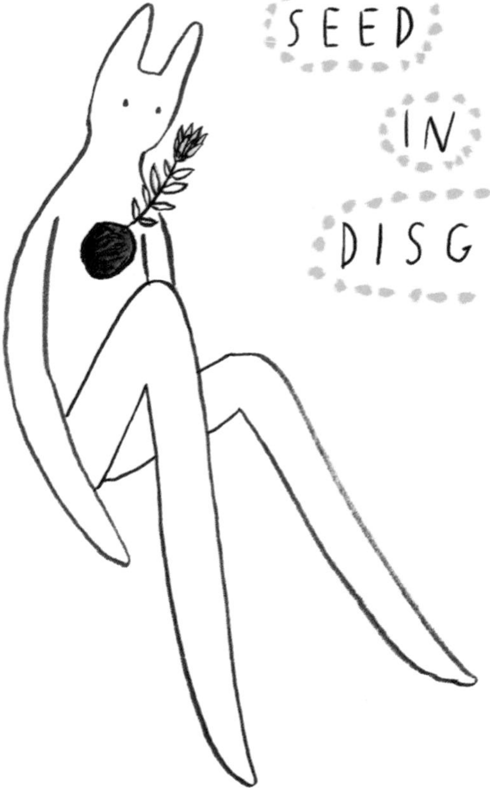

About the Author

Yumi Sakugawa is an Ignatz Award-nominated comic book artist and the author of *I Think I Am In Friend-Love With You* and *Your Illustrated Guide to Becoming One with the Universe*. Her comics have also appeared in *Bitch*, *The Best American Nonrequired Reading 2014*, The Rumpus, *Folio*, *Fjords Review*, and other publications. A graduate from the fine art program of the University of California, Los Angeles, she lives in Los Angeles. Visit her online at www.yumisakugawa.com.